Congratulations!

You've been chosen to make a wedding extra special!

As a Ring Bearer, your job is super important. You'll carry the rings

down the aisle—how cool is that?

Ready to learn more? Let's go!

About me

My name is: _____

I am _____ years old.

My favorite color is:

_____

My favorite superhero is:

_____

I'm excited to be a Ring Bearer because:

_____

I can't wait for the wedding day so I can:

_____

I SPY WEDDING GAME

Count the hearts, notes, and rainbows in the box.

CONNECT THE DOTS

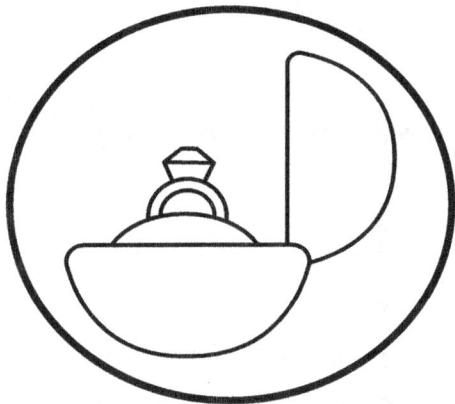

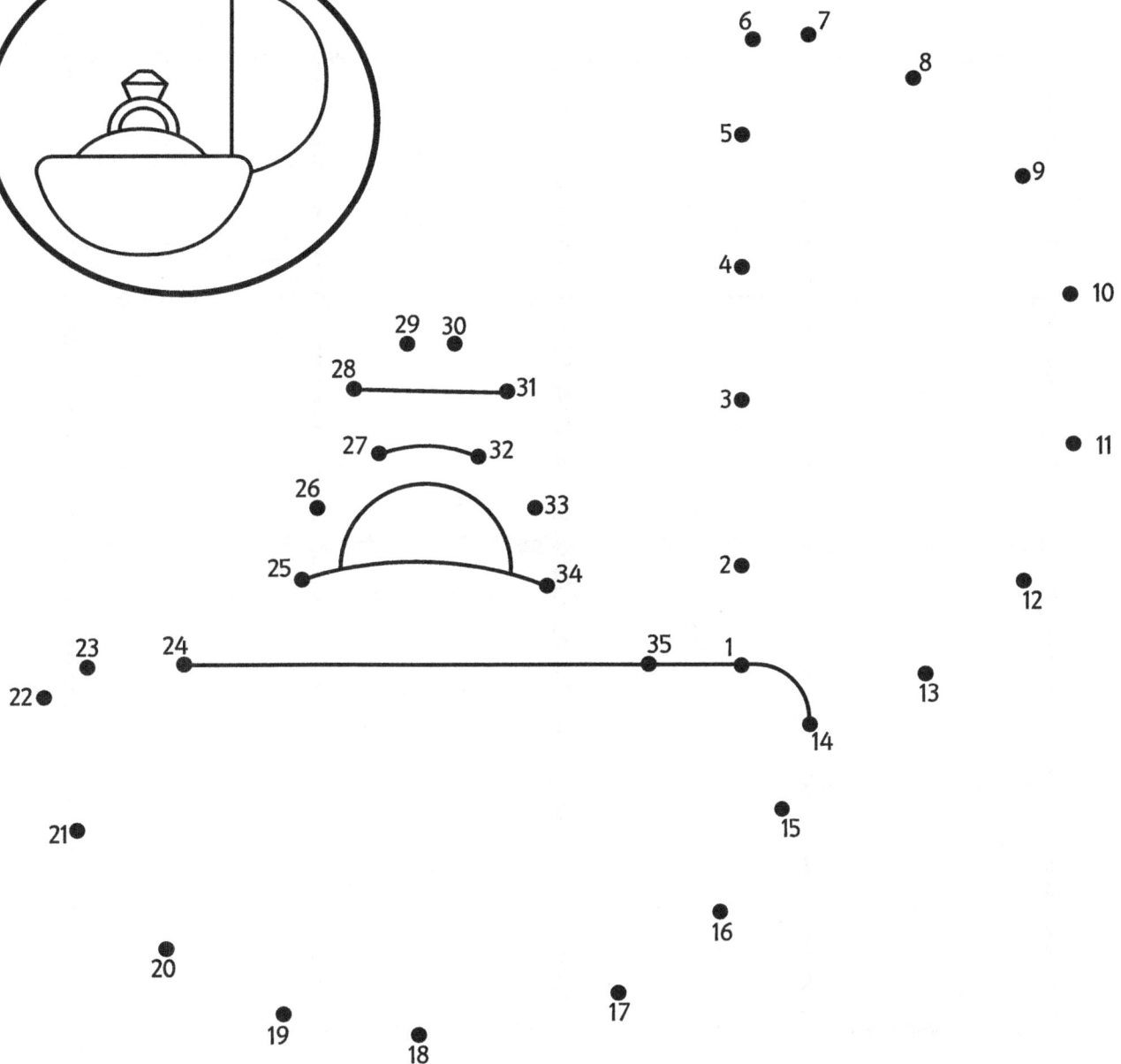

6
7
8
5
9
4
10
29 30
28
31
3
27
32
11
26
33
25
34
2
12
23 24
35 1
22
13
14
21
15
16
20
17
19
18

⊰⊱ **DID YOU KNOW?** ⊰⊱

The groom gives the bride two rings: an engagement ring during the
proposal and a wedding ring during the ceremony.

WEDDING SUDOKU 1

Draw images so they appear only once in every row and column.

DID YOU KNOW?

When a ring bearer receives his invitation, it means he's been asked to play an important role in the couple's special day! The invitation shares the date, time, and place of the wedding, and it means a big day full of fun is coming soon!

SOLVE THE MAZE AND FIND THE CAR KEYS

CUT OUT THE WEDDING INVITATION

TRACE THE CAR FOR THE WEDDING

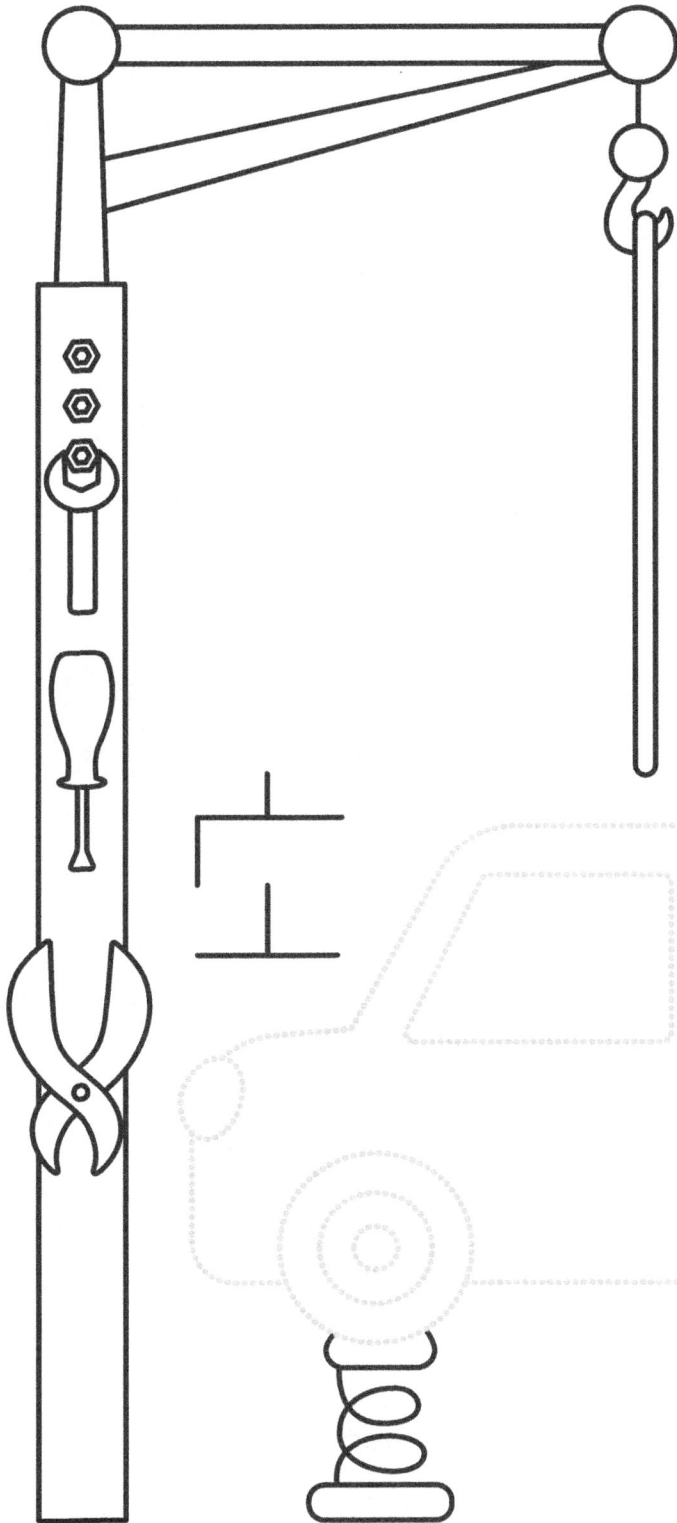

Let's get the car ready for the trip to the wedding!

Trace the car carefully.
Color it to make it cool for the wedding!

CROSSWORD PUZZLE

COUNT HOW MANY?

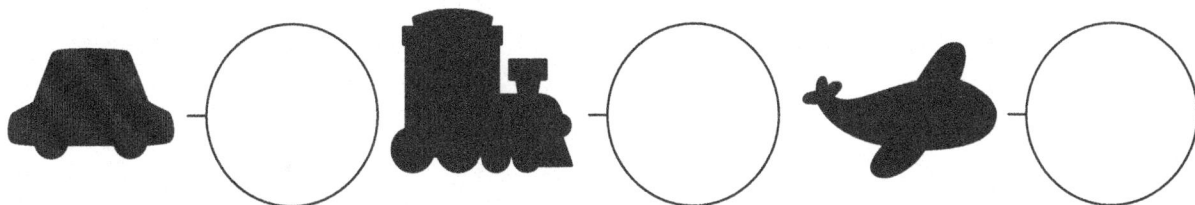

DRAW THE PATH TO THE CHARGING STATION

CROSSWORD PUZZLE

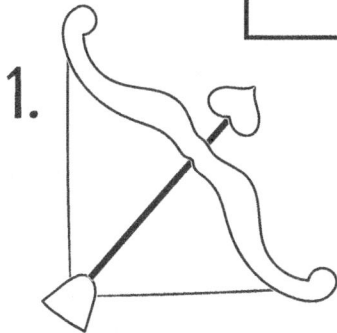

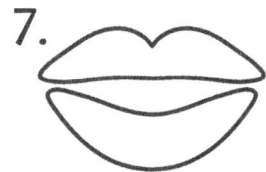

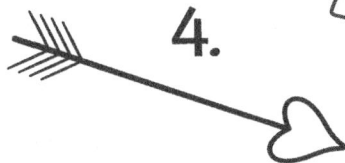

2.

1. 2. 9. 7. 5.

4. 8. 6.

1.

↑5.

5.

7.

6.

8.

4.

9.

3.

WRITING PRACTICE

INVITATION

invitation

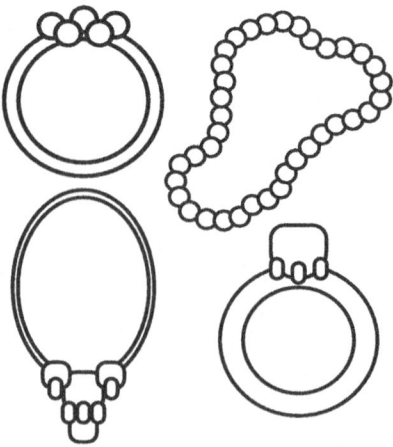

JEWELRY

jewelry

DRAW YOUR RING BEARER OUTFIT

WEDDING SUDOKU 2

Draw images so they appear only once in
every row and column.

COLOR THE GROOM'S ATTIRE

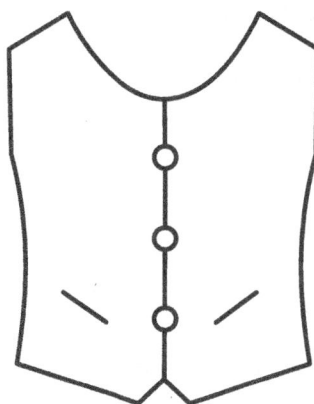

WRITING PRACTICE

GROOM

groom

HAT

hat

MATCHING GAME

Match the wedding locations! Draw a line connecting each place to its correct name.

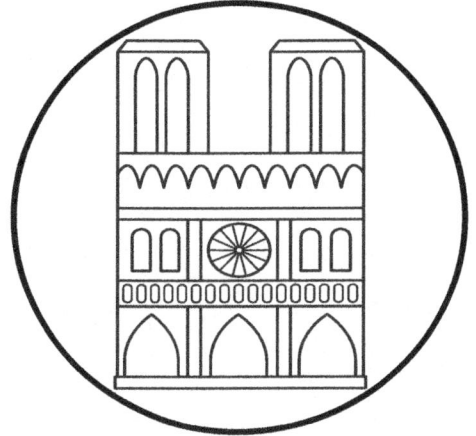

CASTLE

MOSQUE

BEACH

CHURCH

SYNAGOGUE

CITY HALL

FIND THE SHADOW

Find and circle the matching shadow of the groom.

WEDDING RIDDLES

I carry the rings, walking down the aisle. I'm small, but I do it with a smile.

I am _____.

I'm the place where the couple says, "I do." I'm decorated with flowers, just for two.

I am _____.

I walk in front of the bride, tossing petals in the air. I'm small and cute, with flowers to share.

I am _____.

You toss me in the air, then your friends shout. Whoever catches me might be the next to marry, no doubt.

I am _____.

FOLLOW THE CORRECT WAY

Help the white dove find her partner by following the triangles. Color all the triangles blue to guide her on her journey!

SPOT 5 DIFFERENCES

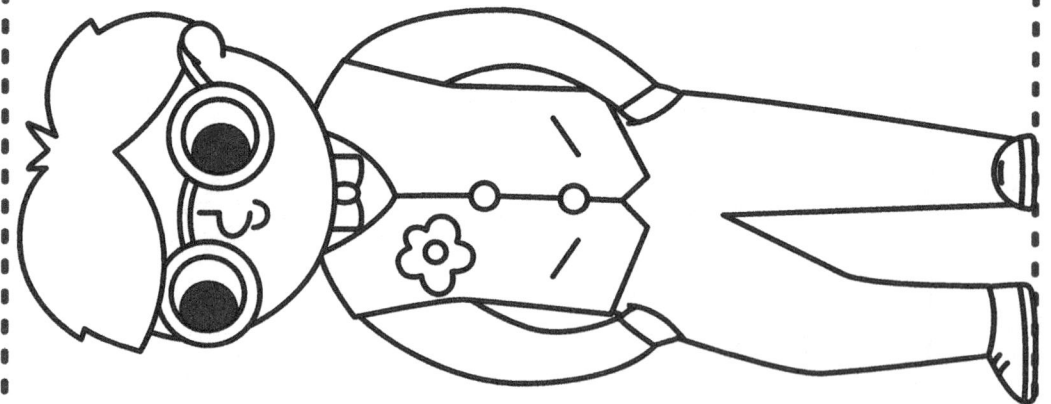

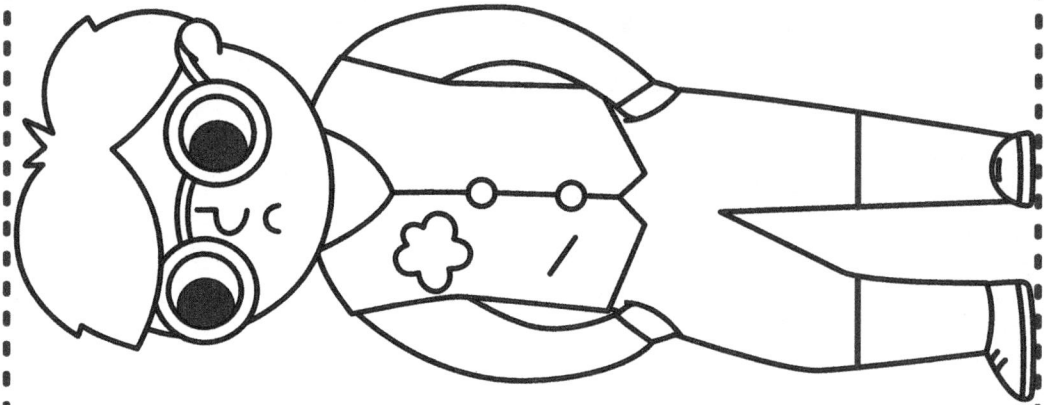

RING BEARER'S MISSION

Your mission (and it's a super important one):

1. Walk down the aisle like a superhero

2. Keep the rings safe on the special pillow

3. Hand the rings carefully to the grown-ups

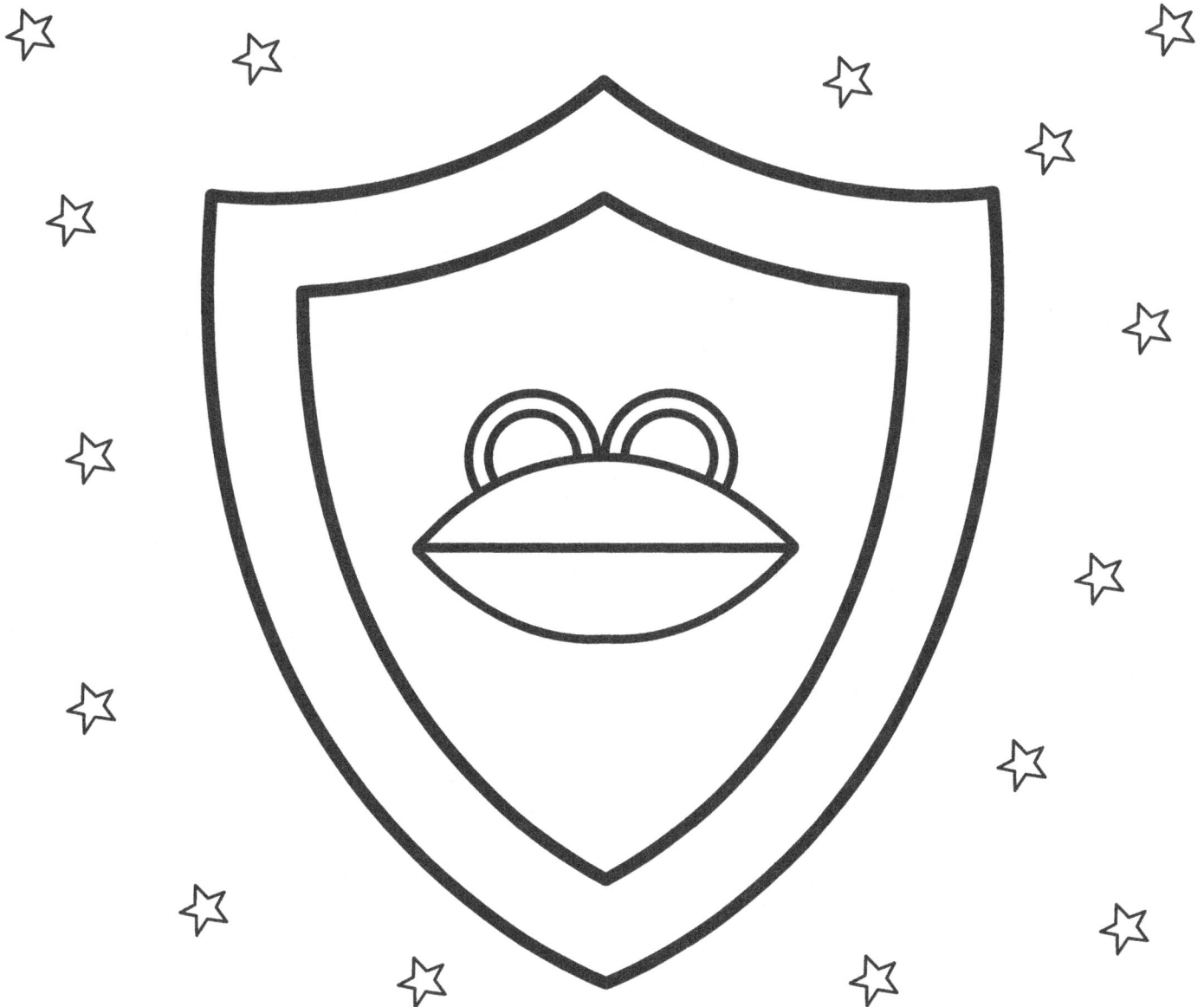

LEFT OR RIGHT

How many to the left? How many to the right?

LEFT _____

RIGHT _____

DID YOU KNOW?

The officiant leads the wedding ceremony while everyone watches silently, helping the couple exchange their vows and rings to become husband and wife.

WEDDING JOKES

What did the bride say to her shoes?

"We're going to take a big step today!"

Why did the bride bring a pencil to the wedding?

Because she wanted to draw some attention!

What did the ring say to the finger?

You're the one I've been waiting for!

COLOR BY NUMBER

1. DARK ORANGE
2. PEACH
3. PINK
4. LAVENDER
5. CREAM
6. BLACK
7. LIGHT BLUE

COUNTING PRACTICE

Count the objects and choose the correct solution.

| 2 | 1 | 5 | 9 |

| 9 | 4 | 3 | 8 |

| 1 | 4 | 2 | 8 |

| 9 | 7 | 2 | 3 |

WEDDING RIDDLES

I'm a song everyone knows. At weddings, I play as the bride

walks slow.

I am _____.

I'm worn by the bride and flow like a dream. I'm white, fluffy,

and part of the team.

I am _____.

I play sweet music while the couple dances. I set the mood for

all the romances.

I am _____.

I hold a tasty surprise, with frosting on top. You cut into me at

the reception—chop, chop!

I am _____.

SPOT 10 DIFFERENCES

DID YOU KNOW?

The ring bearer has an important job: carrying the wedding rings on a special pillow or in a box while walking down the aisle before the flower girl. He makes sure the rings are safe for the bride and groom!

LET'S COUNT

Count the objects and choose the correct solution.

| 8 | 1 | 2 | 9 |

| 7 | 4 | 3 | 8 |

| 3 | 1 | 6 | 8 |

| 9 | 7 | 1 | 3 |

COLOR BY NUMBER

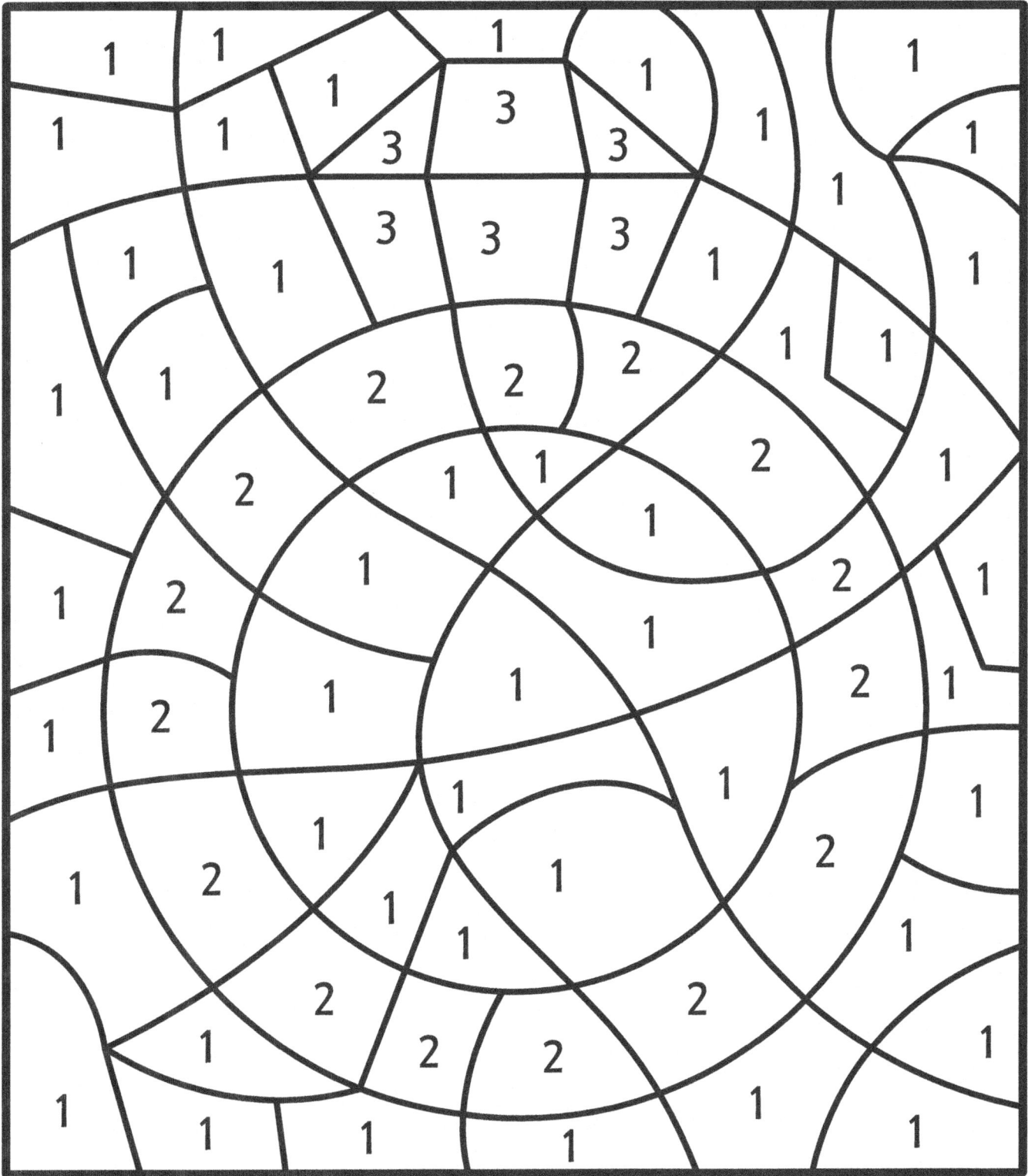

1. PURPLE   2. YELLOW   3. RED

WRITING PRACTICE

OFFICIANT

officiant

PRESENT

present

CONNECT THE DOTS

‹—❦❀ **DID YOU KNOW** ❀❦—›

Before the big day, you'll practice walking down the aisle and
handing over the rings so you'll be ready to help the Bride and
Groom with their special moment!

FIND THE THIEF WHO STOLE THE RING

WHO DOESN'T BELONG?

CHOOSE NUMBERS
IN ORDER

WHAT DO YOU NEED TO CATCH THE THIEF

Circle and color the items you would use to catch a thief.

COLOR THE LETTERS

Color any letters that are in the Bride's name.

A J B L X
I
H T K S E G
D F N
O Q R
C U
V W P Y Z M

Write the name:

_____

DRAW THE RING ON THE GRID

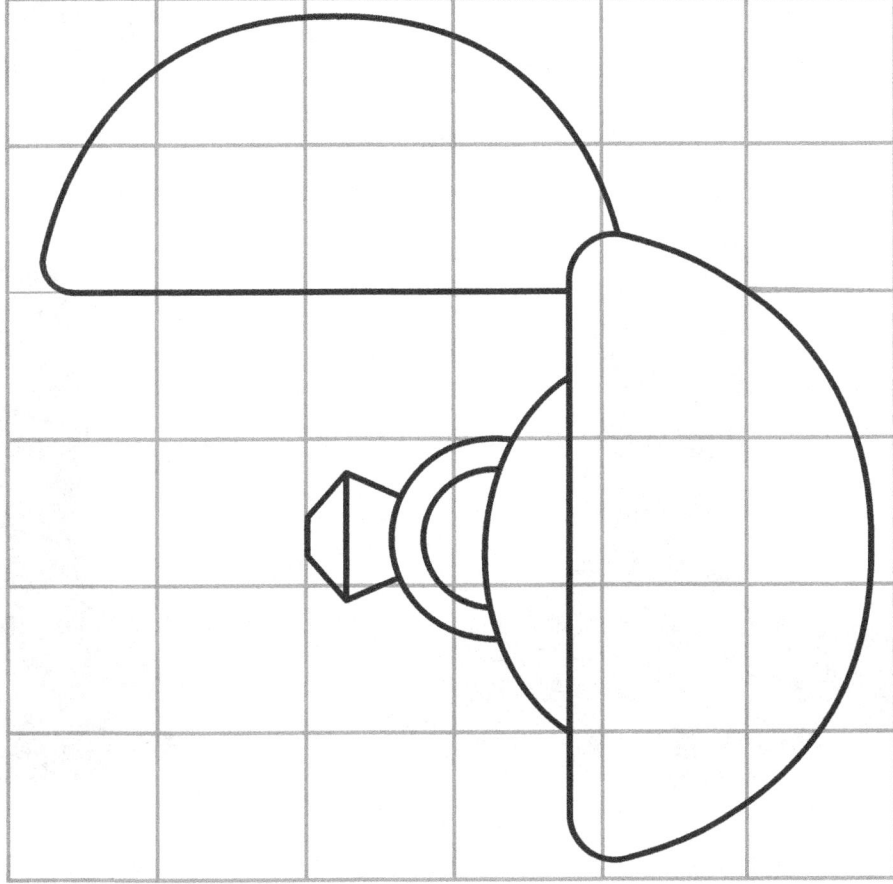

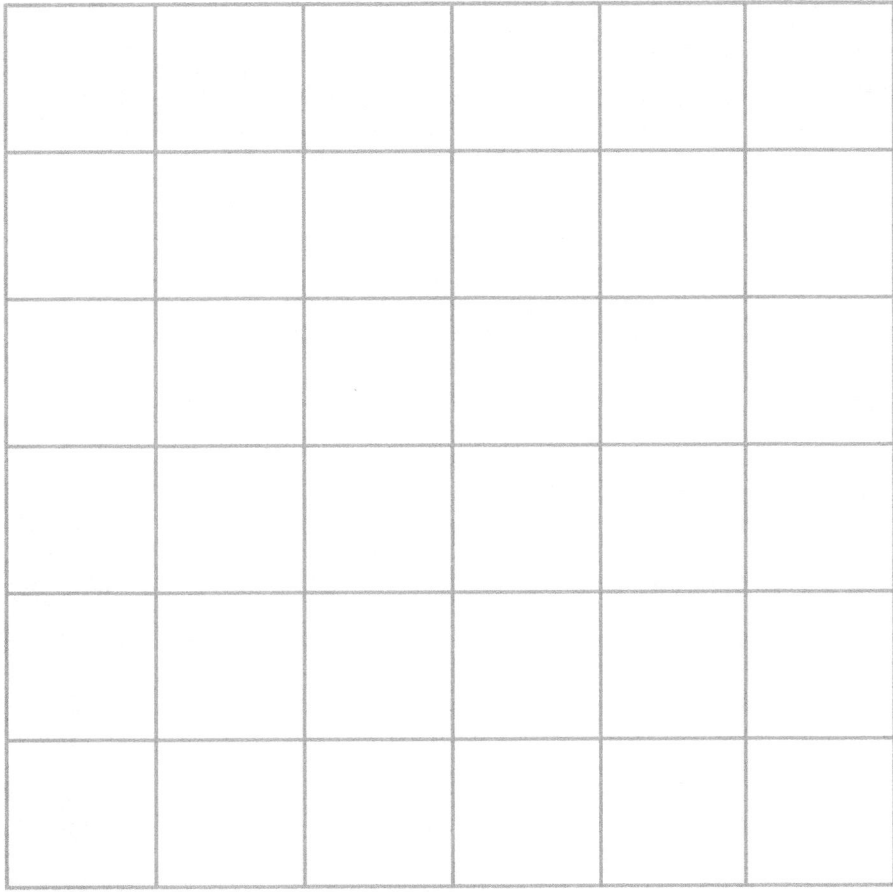

FIND THE SHADOW

Find and circle the correct shadow of the bride.

WEDDING MAZE

Help the flower girl find her way out of the maze.

CONNECT THE DOTS

Connect the dots and color the cute wedding bird.

DID YOU KNOW?

The flower girl walks down the aisle before the bride. She might carry a pretty bouquet or sprinkle flower petals

WHO IS THE WINNER OF THE RACE?

RING BEARER

or

FLOWER GIRL

WEDDING CEREMONY

Color the image of the married couple.

DID YOU KNOW?

When the bride and groom exchange rings, it shows their love and promise to be together! Everyone stays quiet while the officiant, bride, and groom speak.

FIND THE SHADOW

Find and circle the correct shadow of the wedding couple.

WEDDING RIDDLES

I'm tiny and sweet and thrown in the air. At weddings, I'm

tossed to show people care.

I am _____.

I'm a piece of paper, signed by two. I prove the wedding day was

true.

I am _____.

I'm round and shiny, and I fit on your finger.

I'm a symbol of love that will always linger.

I am _____.

I wear a tuxedo and wait at the end of the aisle. I'm so happy to

see my bride walk down with a smile.

I am _____.

WEDDING VOWS

Wedding vows are like super important promises the bride and groom make to each other. The couple promises to be a team forever, helping each other out and always having each other's back.

Write down the cool promises you heard them make at the wedding – like promising to be best friends forever, to help each other fight life's battles, and to be each other's biggest fan no matter what!

WRITING PRACTICE

KEY   KEY

key   key

LOVE LOVE

love love

CHOOSE NUMBERS FROM 1 TO 20

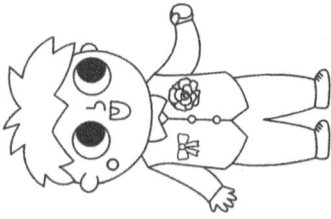

9	7	6	8	11	7	3	2	1
12	14	13	12	14	8	4	5	1	11	4
17	16	15	14	12	11	10	3	5	1	5
19	18	17	16	13	7	9	7	3	2	7
20	16	18	15	14	5	8	9	4	7	9
		19	11	10	15	7	6	5	9	11
		17	18	17	16	9	4	8	11	9

CAN YOU DRAW THE WEDDING COUPLE

FUN WITH COUNTING AND TRACING

Enjoy the process of counting and tracing numbers.

 One One One

 Two Two Two

 Three Three

 Four Four Four

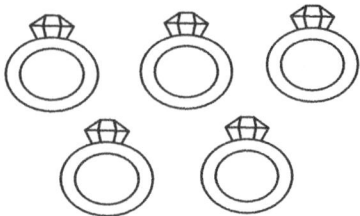 Five Five Five

DOT TO DOT EXERCISE

DID YOU KNOW?

After saying 'I do,' the bride and groom share a kiss! This tradition
started long ago as a way to show their love and seal their promise.

WEDDING JOKES

Why did the bride wear sunglasses?

Because her future was so bright!

Why did the groom get cold feet?

Because he forgot his wedding socks!

Why did the groom bring a ruler to the wedding?

Because he wanted everything to measure up!

COLOR BY NUMBER

1. LIGHT BLUE   3. PINK   5. BROWN   7. GREEN
2. LAVENDER   4. BLACK   6. YELLOW   8. CREAM

WEDDING DANCE

DID YOU KNOW?

The first dance is a special moment at the wedding where the bride and groom dance together in front of their guests.

What song is played during the first dance? Write it down below.

DID YOU KNOW?

Weddings have lots of yummy food for everyone to enjoy! There are tasty snacks and meals to make the guests happy and full.

STARTING LETTERS

Carefully look at these pictures and circle the correct letter.

I		NVITATION
O		

V		ANDLE
C		

G		ROOM
V		

F		RESENT
P		

WEDDING DANCE

Cake cutting is a wedding tradition where the bride and groom share their first slice, symbolizing their unity. They often feed each other a bite before serving the cake to guests.

WEDDING CAKE MAZE

Can you find your way out of the maze?

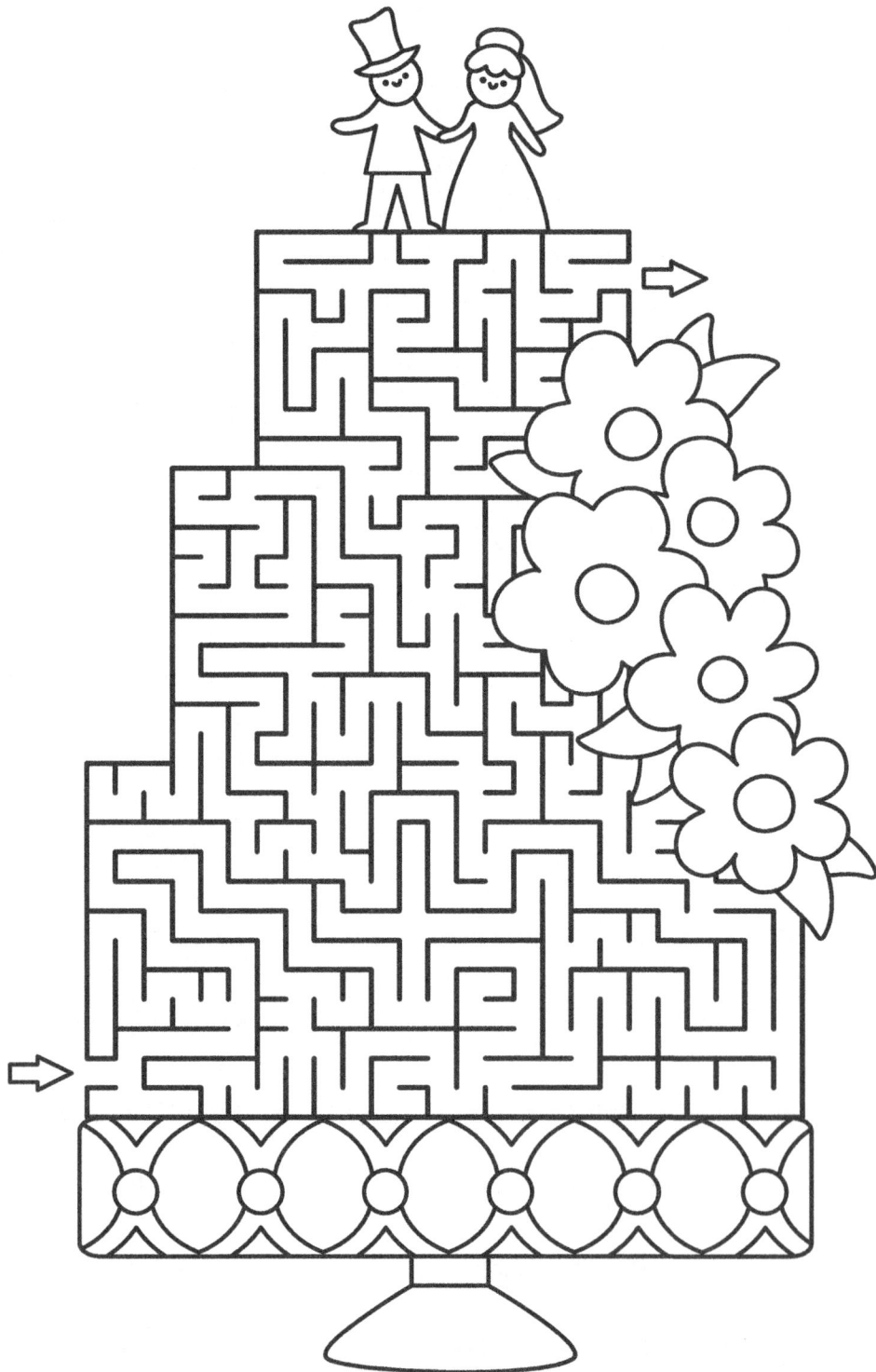

WEDDING JOKES

Why did the couple invite a cow to their wedding?

Because they wanted a moo-special guest!

Why did the couple bring a map to their big day?

Because they didn't want to lose their way down the aisle!

Why did the ring get nervous at the wedding?

It was afraid of getting wrapped up!

COUNT THE ITEMS

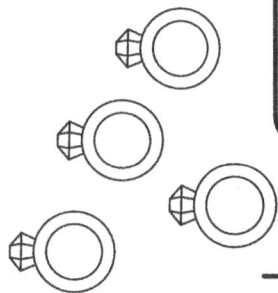

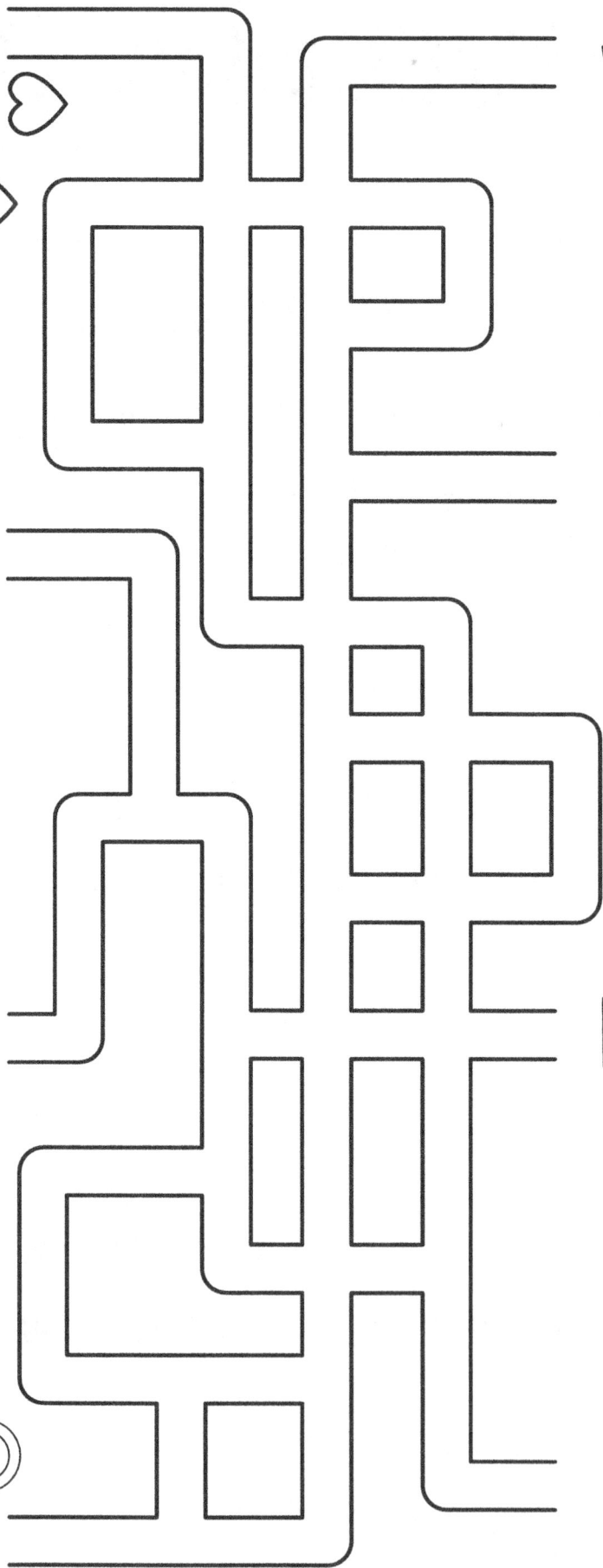

WEDDING SCAVENGER HUNT CARDS

Groom	Suit	Balloon
Drinks	Gift	Candle
Hat	Fireworks	Sunglasses

WEDDING JOKES

What did one flower say to the other flower at the wedding?
"I hope we end up in the same bouquet!"

What's the bride's favorite kind of music?
Something old, something new, something borrowed, something blues!

Why did the ring bearer bring a flashlight?
To make sure he didn't lose the rings!

WHAT ARE THEY MISSING

WRITING PRACTICE

CAKE

cake

DRESS

dress

FUN WITH COUNTING AND TRACING

Enjoy the process of counting and tracing numbers.

 Six Six Six Six

 Seven Seven

 Eight Eight

 Nine Nine Nine

 Ten Ten Ten

FIND THE PRESENT

WRITING PRACTICE

UNDERWEAR

underwear

VEIL   VEIL

veil   veil

CONNECT THE DOTS

Connect the dots and color the wedding car.

─── ❧ ❧ **DID YOU KNOW?** ❧ ❧ ───

A honeymoon is a special trip for newlyweds to celebrate their marriage, often at destinations like tropical beaches or charming cities.

DRAW THE PLANE

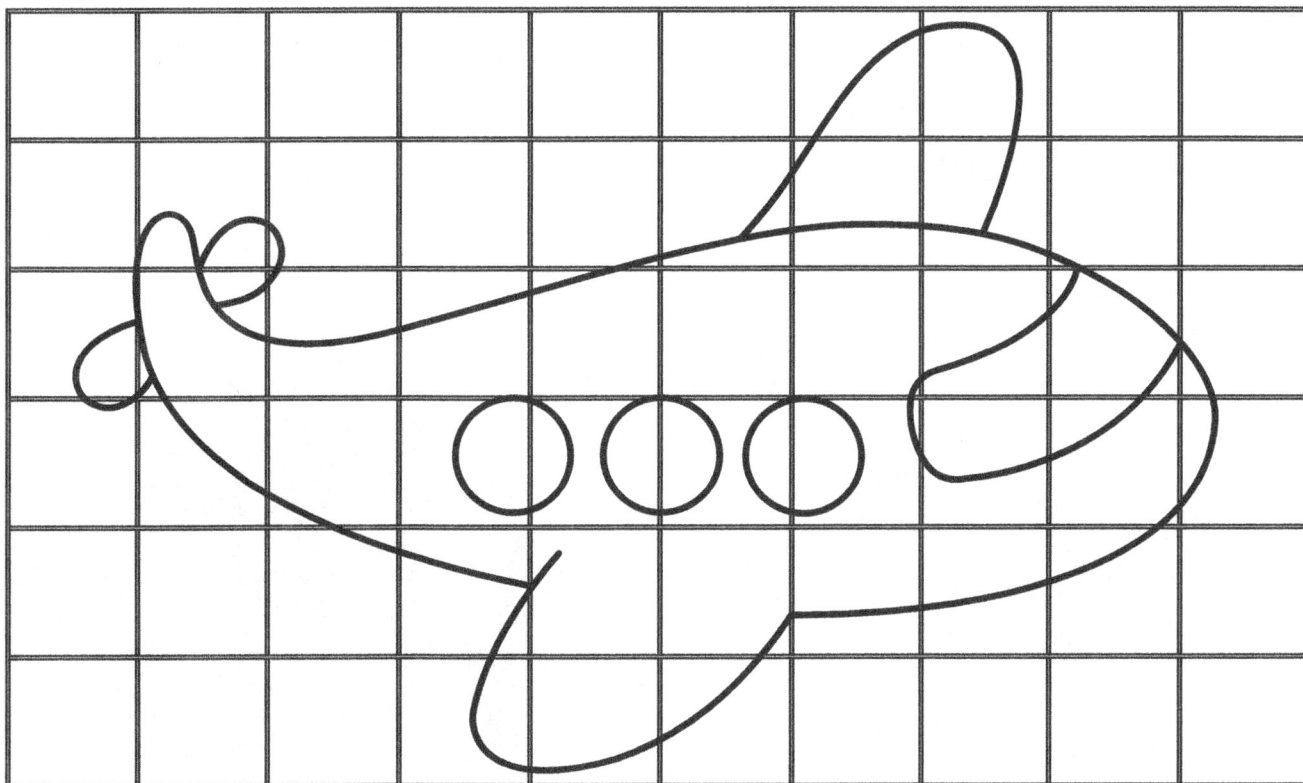

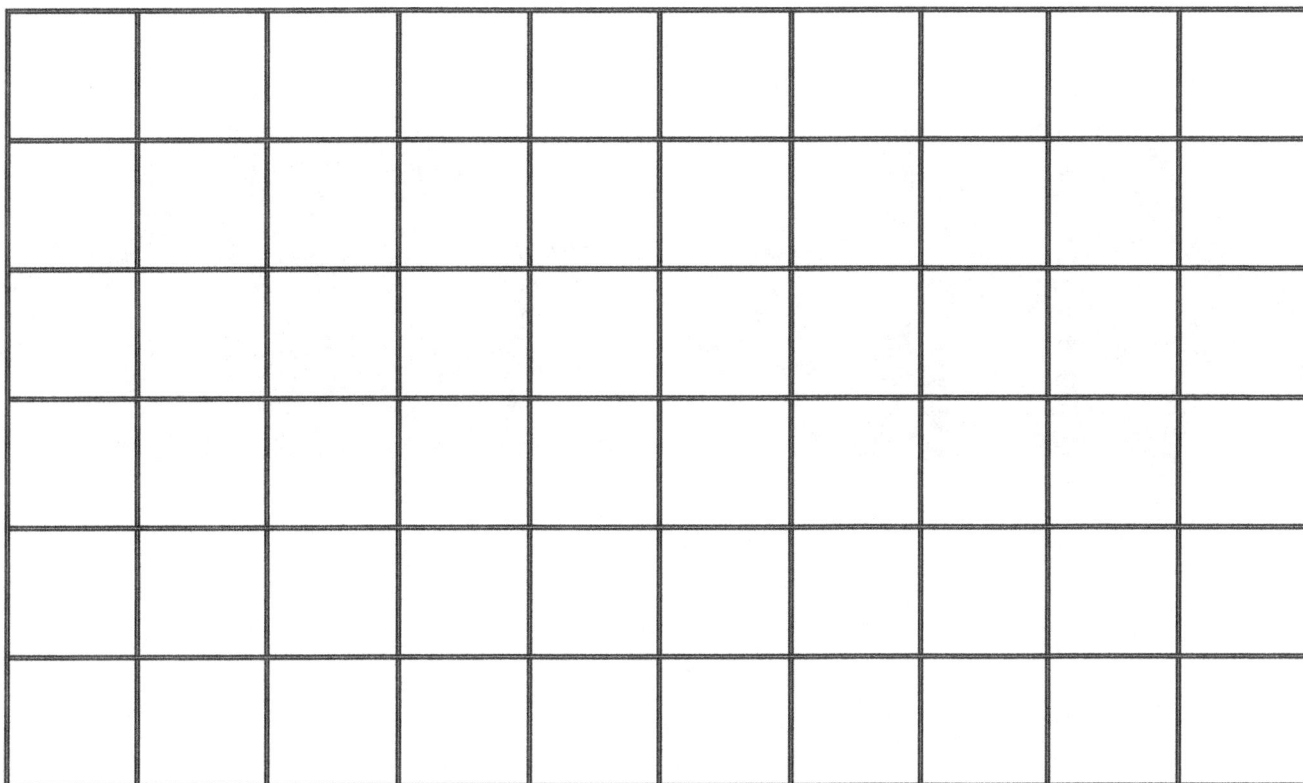

FIND THE SHADOW

Find and circle the matching shadow of a wedding car.

WRITING PRACTICE

SHOE SHOE

shoe shoe

TIE TIE

tie tie

FIND THE SHADOW

Find and circle the correct shadow of the wedding couple heading on their honeymoon.

TIC – TAC – TOE

Play these games of noughts and crosses with a friend.

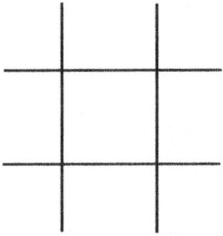

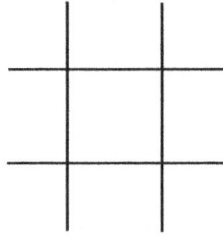

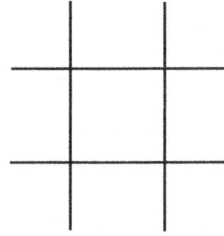

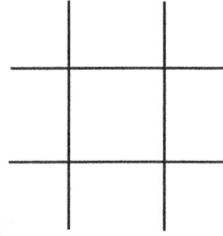

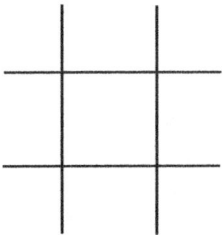

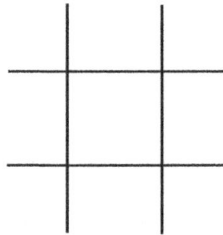

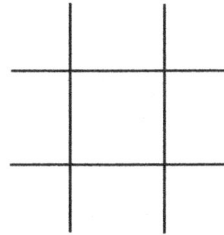

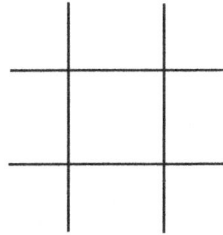

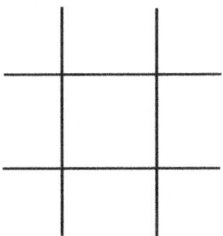

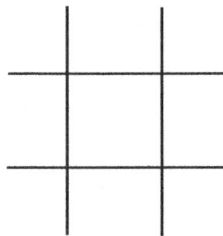

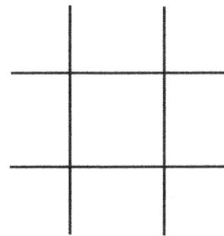

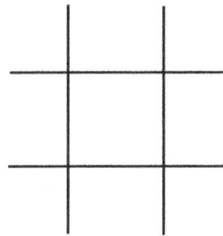

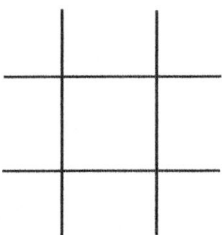

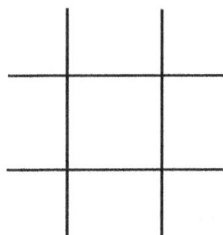

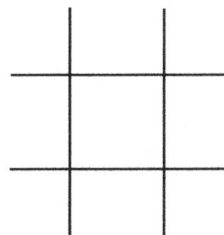

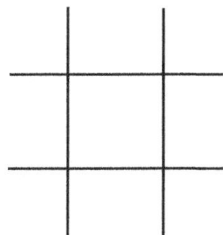

DECODE THE MESSAGE

Write the word according to the code.

A	B	C	D	E	F	G	H	I	J	K	L	M

N	O	P	Q	R	S	T	U	V	W	X	Y	Z

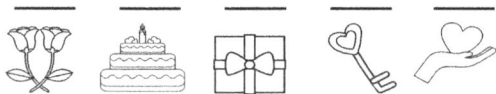

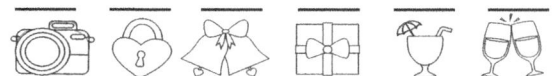

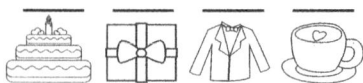

FIND THE PAIR

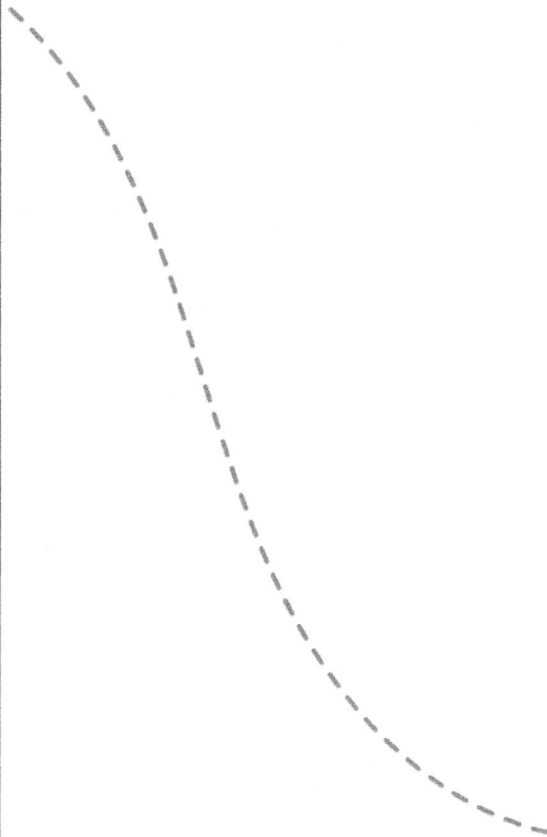

FIND TWO SAME PRESENTS

WRITING PRACTICE

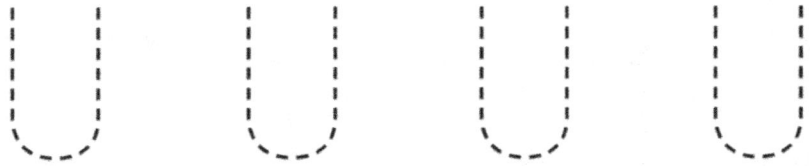

UNDERWEAR

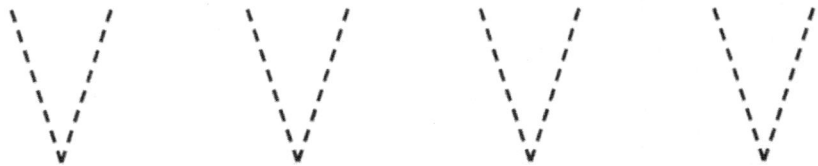

VEIL

WEDDING CAKE

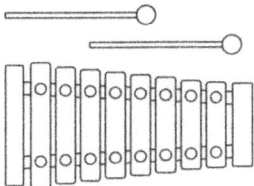

XYLOPHONE

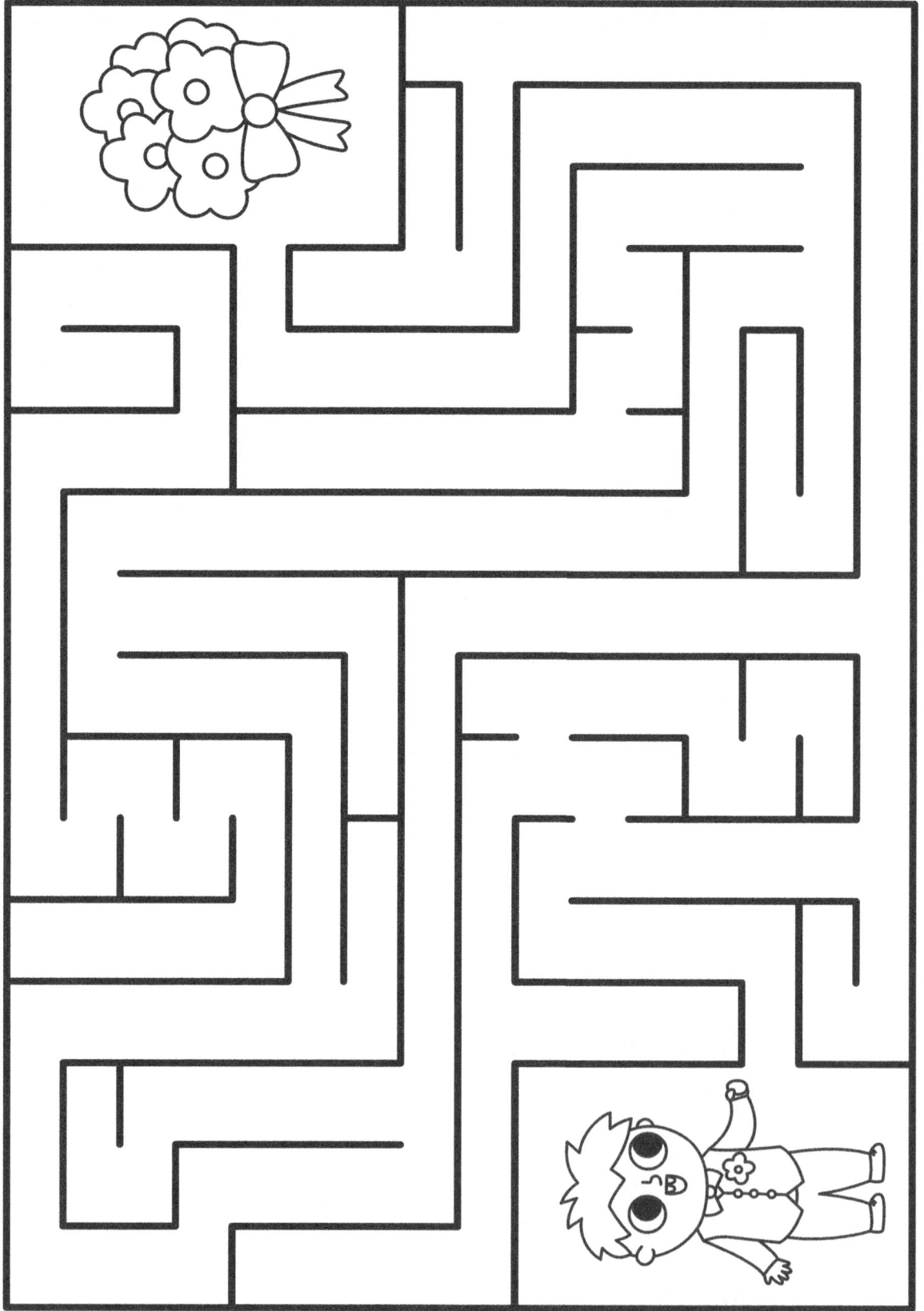

RING BEARER'S MAZE PATH

FIND THE MISSING ITEMS

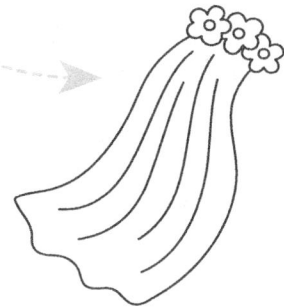

WORD SCRAMBLE

DERIB

☐ ☐ ☐ ☐ ☐

OMROG

☐ ☐ ☐ ☐ ☐

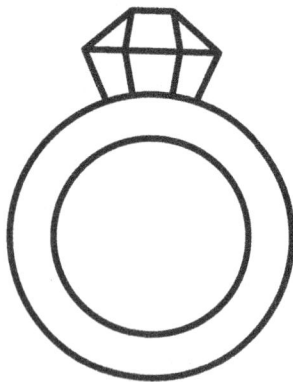

GRIN

☐ ☐ ☐ ☐

FIND THE PAIR

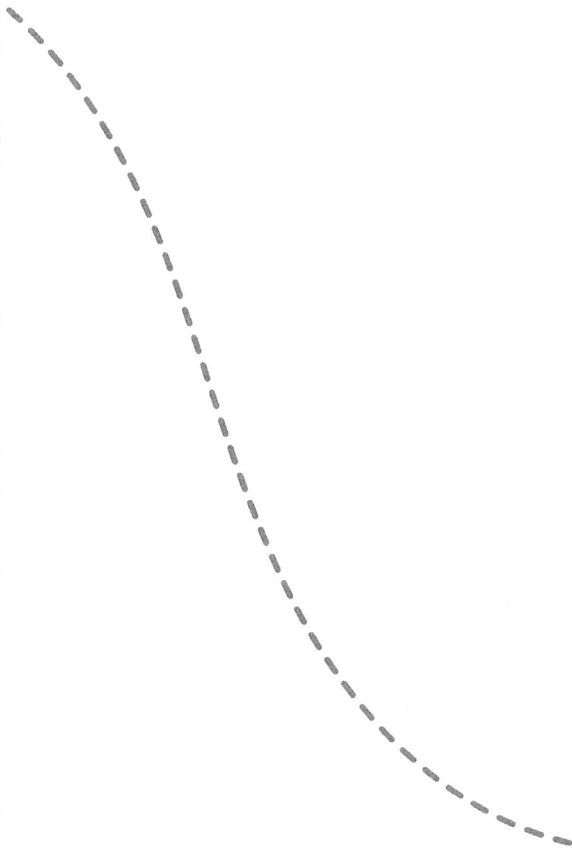

DOT TO DOT EXERCISE

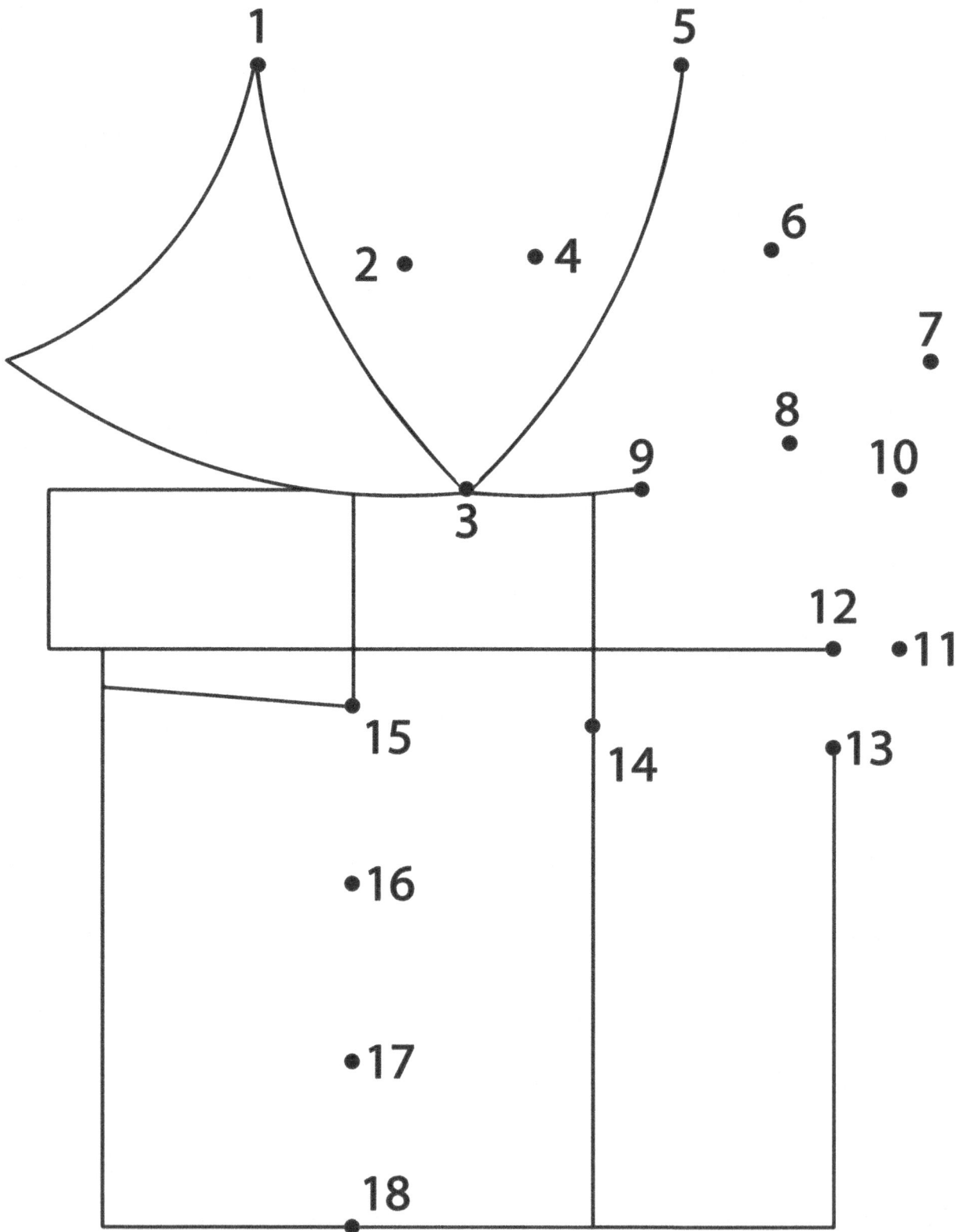

1

5

2

4

6

7

8

9

10

3

12

11

15

13

14

16

17

18

TRACE THE LINE

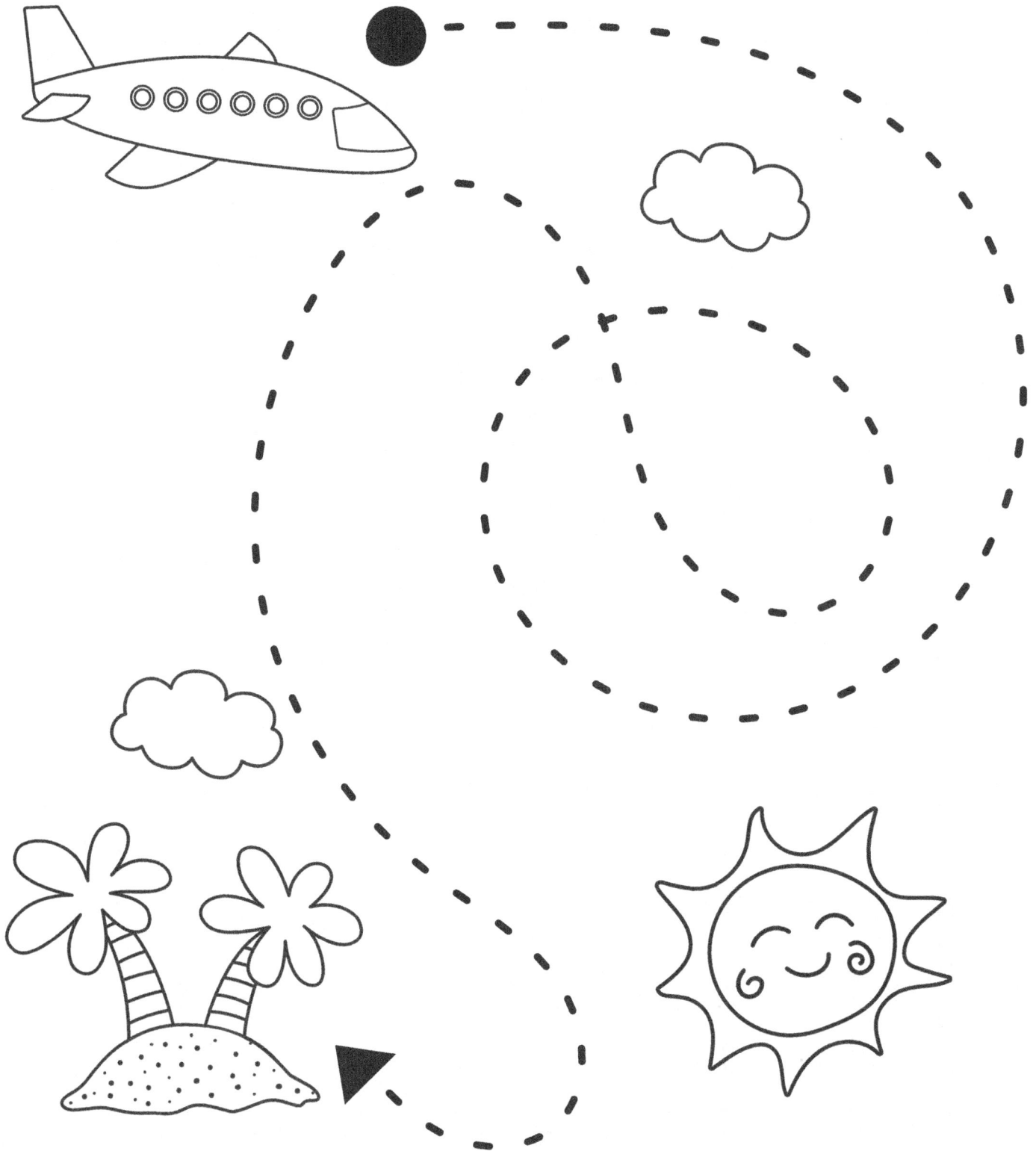

SOLVE THE MAZE

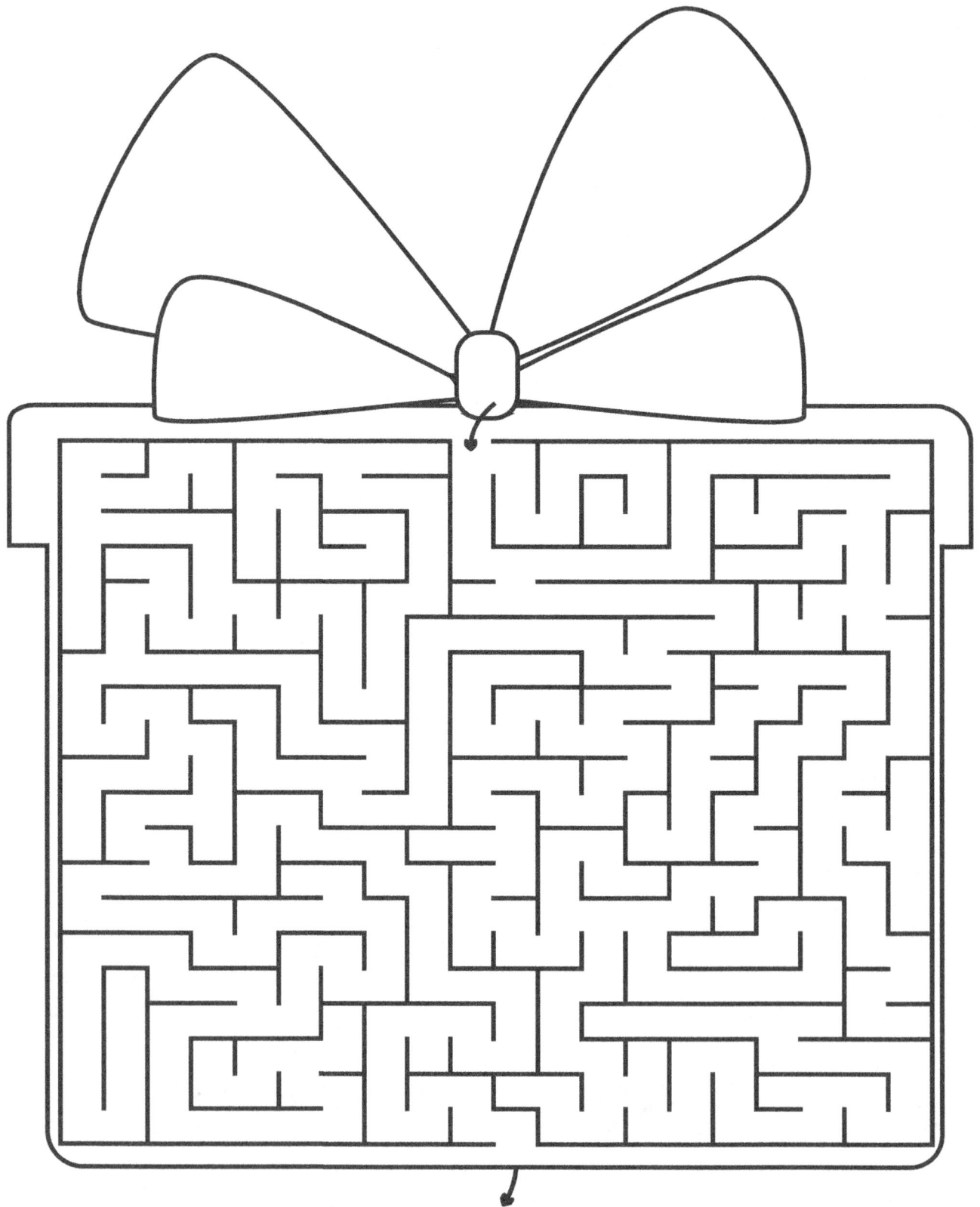

MORE, LESS OR EQUAL

Choose the correct answer.

<   >   =

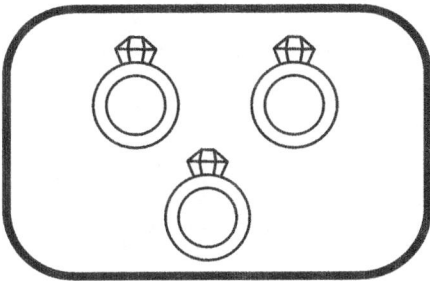  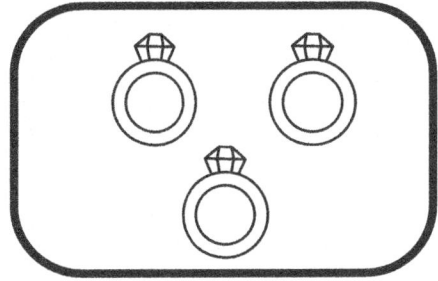

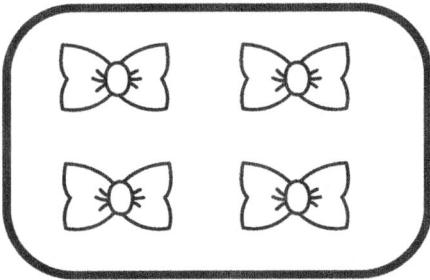 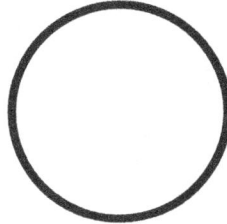 

 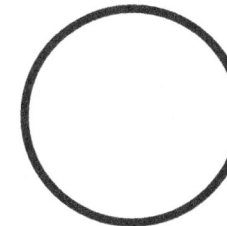 

 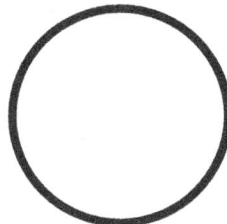 

COLOR THE LETTERS

Color any letters that are in the Groom's name.

A J I B L X
H T K S E G
O Q R D F N
V W P Y Z C U M

Write the name:

_____

LEFT OR RIGHT

How many to the left? How many to the right?

_____
LEFT

_____
RIGHT

WRITING PRACTICE

EARRINGS

earrings

FLOWERS

flowers

SPOT 4 DIFFERENCES

MY RING BEARER

Check out all the fun things you do as a Ring Bearer.
Follow the path, match the pictures, and color the drawings!

START

1

Get dressed

2

Arrive at the wedding

ADVENTURE

4

☐ Hand the rings to the best man or the officiant

Mr. Mrs.

5

☐ Sit quietly with my family and enjoy the wedding

3

☐ Carry the ring pillow carefully down the aisle

FINISH

☐ Have fun!!

— My memories —

My favorite part of the wedding was:

_____

_____

The coolest thing I saw at the wedding was:

_____

My favorite memory from the wedding is:

_____

_____

The best thing about being a Ring Bearer was:

_____

Note of thanks for the Ring Bearer

from the

wedding couple

Congratulations!

You did it!

Every activity is complete—you're a true

Ring Bearer superstar!

Solutions

WEDDING SUDOKU 1

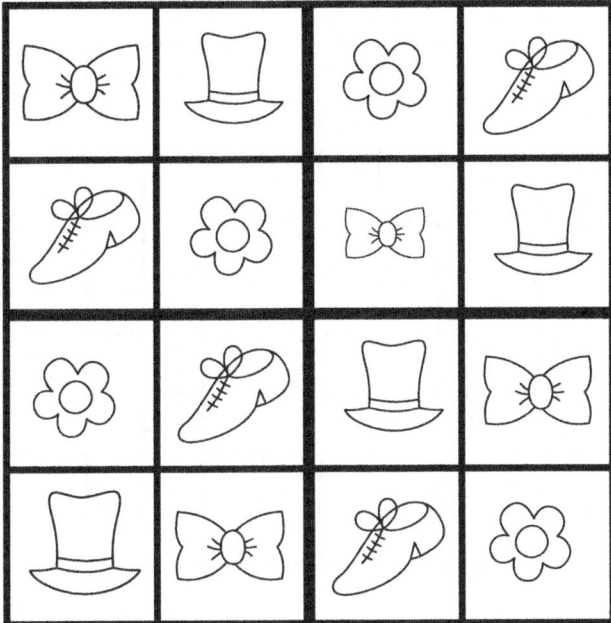

SOLVE THE MAZE AND FIND A RING

WEDDING SUDOKU 2

SPOT 5 DIFFERENCES

SPOT 10 DIFFERENCES

FIND THE THIEF WHO STOLE THE RING

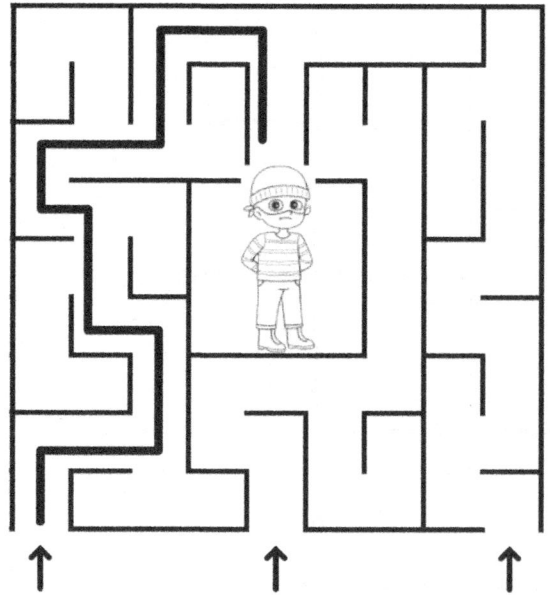

WEDDING MAZE

Help the flower girl find her way out of the maze.

WHO IS THE WINNER OF THE RACE?

RING BEARER
or
FLOWER GIRL

WEDDING CAKE MAZE

COUNT THE ITEMS AND FIND THE WAY

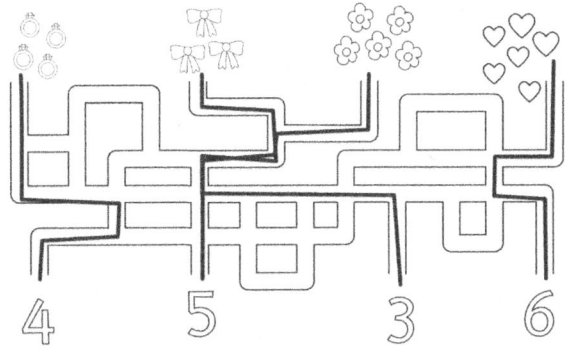

4   5   3   6

FIND THE PRESENT

FIND THE PAIR

FIND TWO SAME PRESENTS

RING BEARER'S MAZE PATH

SOLVE THE MAZE

SPOT 4 DIFFERENCES

Thank you for choosing this book!

I greatly appreciate the time you took to color and explore the pages.

As a small indie publisher, it means a lot.

I'd love to hear your thoughts on Amazon. Even a brief review is incredibly helpful.

To leave your feedback:

1. Open your camera app

2. Point your mobile phone device at the QR code bellow.

3. The review page will appear in your web browser

or open the following link:

https://mybook.to/9a5js

Made in United States
North Haven, CT
02 June 2025